TULSA CITY-COUNTY LIBRARY

W9-COD-159

I Love Sports

Gymnastics

by Allan Morey

Bullfrog Books

Ideas for Parents and Teachers

Bullfrog Books let children practice reading informational text at the earliest reading levels. Repetition, familiar words, and photo labels support early readers.

Before Reading

- Discuss the cover photo. What does it tell them?
- Look at the picture glossary together. Read and discuss the words.

Read the Book

- "Walk" through the book and look at the photos. Let the child ask questions. Point out the photo labels.
- Read the book to the child, or have him or her read independently.

After Reading

- Prompt the child to think more. Ask: Have you ever tried gymnastics? Have you ever watched a meet? Which event was your favorite?

Bullfrog Books are published by Jump!
5357 Penn Avenue South
Minneapolis, MN 55419
www.jumplibrary.com

Copyright © 2015 Jump! International copyright reserved in all countries. No part of this book may be reproduced in any form without written permission from the publisher.

Library of Congress Cataloging-in-Publication Data

Morey, Allan.
  Gymnastics / by Allan Morey.
    pages cm. — (I love sports)
Summary: "This photo-illustrated book for early readers introduces the basics of gymnastics and encourages kids to try it. Includes labeled diagram of gymnastics equipment and photo glossary."
— Provided by publisher.
  Includes index.
  Audience: Age: 5.
  Audience: Grade: K to Grade 3.
  ISBN 978-1-62031-179-0 (hardcover) —
  ISBN 978-1-62496-266-0 (ebook)
1. Gymnastics for children—Juvenile literature.
I. Title.
GV464.5.H62 2015
796.44—dc23
                                        2014032128

Series Editor: Rebecca Glaser
Series Designer: Ellen Huber
Book Designer: Michelle Sonnek
Photo Researcher: Michelle Sonnek

Photo Credits: All photos by Shutterstock except: age fotostock, 11; Alamy, 6–7, 23br; Corbis, 8–9, 14–15, 20–21, 23bl; Getty, 16–17, 22, 23tr; iStock, 5, 22, 24; SuperStock, 10, 22; Thinkstock, 4, 18.

Printed in the United States of America at Corporate Graphics in North Mankato, Minnesota.

Table of Contents

Let's Tumble!

Get on the mat.

Jump. Roll. And flip.
Let's do gymnastics!

Today there is a meet.
Kids go to the gym.
They will compete.

Kira is on the balance beam.
She hops. She turns.
She does not fall.

Tod is on the rings.

He holds
himself up.

He is strong.

Cari runs up to the vault.
She springs into the air.
She lands on the mat.
Thump!

vault

Juan does the floor exercise.

He rolls on the mat.

Then he does a cartwheel.

cartwheel · · · ▶

15

Judges watch.

They give out scores.

score

Leah has the
best score!

18

She wins.

She gets a medal.

Do you want to try?

Hop. Spin. And tumble.

Gymnastics is fun!

At the Gym

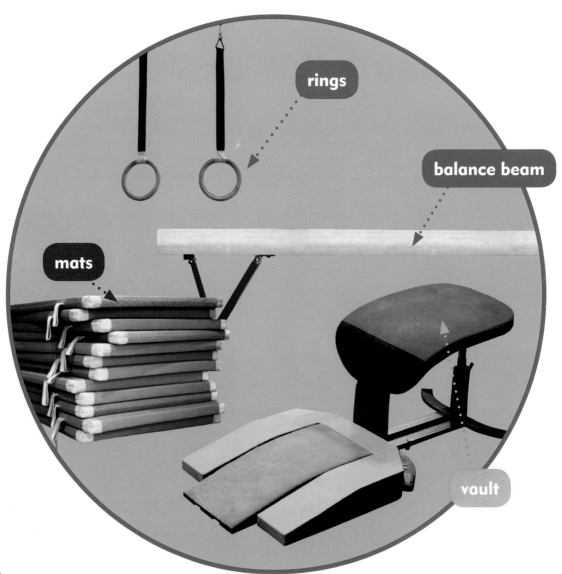

rings

balance beam

mats

vault

Picture Glossary

cartwheel
A move in which the hands touch the ground, the legs go in the air, and one foot lands at a time.

judge
A person who scores how well a gymnast does.

compete
To try hard to outdo others at a sporting event.

medal
An award for doing well.

floor exercise
A gymnastics event performed on a mat without any equipment.

meet
A group of sporting events on one day, where many gymnasts compete against each other.

Index

To Learn More

Learning more is as easy as 1, 2, 3.

1) Go to www.factsurfer.com

2) Enter "gymnastics" into the search box.

3) Click the "Surf" button to see a list of websites.

With factsurfer.com, finding more information is just a click away.